The author is indebted to Dr. Sidney Berger, a rare books librarian
and scholar of the hand-printed book, who read the original manuscript
of this work and made valuable suggestions to the text.

The illustrations were done in pen and ink and painted with watercolor and
gouache. They were inspired by fifteenth-century illuminated
manuscripts and printed works by Jean Fouquet (1420–1481)
and Jan van Eyck (ca. 1395–ca. 1441), especially his
Portrait of a Man in a Turban, painted in 1433.

The Hebrew is Ecclesiastes 3:1; the page of set type is Genesis 1:1–1:31;
the illuminated page and facing page are based on the Göttingen Gutenberg
Bible, End of Prologue and Genesis 1:1–1:31; the verse
Johannes Gutenberg is typesetting is John 1:1.
The typeface used in this book is Post Mediaeval.

For Jack Reisland

Copyright © 2012 by James Rumford
A Neal Porter Book
Published by Flash Point, an imprint of Roaring Brook Press
Roaring Brook Press is a division of Holtzbrinck Publishing Holdings Limited Partnership
175 Fifth Avenue, New York, New York 10010
mackids.com

Library of Congress Cataloging-in-Publication Data
Rumford, James, 1948–
    From the good mountain : how Gutenberg changed the world / James Rumford.
— 1st ed.
    p. cm.
"A Neal Porter Book."
Includes bibliographical references and index.
ISBN 978-1-59643-542-1 (alk. paper)

1. Gutenberg, Johann, 1397?–1468—Juvenile literature. 2. Printing—History—
Origin and antecedents—Juvenile literature. 3. Books—History—Juvenile literature.
4. Printers—Germany—Biography—Juvenile literature. I. Title.
Z126.Z7R77 2012
686.2092—dc23
[B]

                                                                    2011033796

Roaring Brook Press books are available for special promotions and premiums.
For details contact: Director of Special Markets, Holtzbrinck Publishers.

First edition 2012
Printed in China by Toppan Lee Fung Printing Co. Ltd., Dongguan City, Guangdong Province
1   3   5   7   9   10   8   6   4   2

JAMES RUMFORD

From the Good Mountain

HOW GUTENBERG CHANGED THE WORLD

A NEAL PORTER BOOK
ROARING BROOK PRESS
NEW YORK

In the city of Mainz in Germany, around the year 1450, there appeared a mysterious thing. It was made of rags and bones, soot and seeds. It wore a dark brown coat and was filled with gold. It took lead and tin, strong oak, and a mountain to make it.

What was it?

The rags came from beggars' clothes, ladies' pettycoats, and the shirts of gentlemen. The rags were torn and shredded. They were washed and beaten to a pulp. The pulp was poured like porridge into a giant vat where a screen scooped it up into thin sheets. The sheets were pressed and dried, then dipped into a liquid of warm glue that was made of bones, hides, horns, and hooves. The sheets were pressed again and dried. Stiff with glue, they crackled and they rattled in the breeze.

What was this thing
made of rags and bones?

the papermaker's screen

It was paper, and it was ready.

The dark coat came from the skins of goats in the craggy mountains. The skins were cleaned and scraped. They were soaked and stretched and scraped again until all the hair was gone. Then the skins were thrown in a pit of foul-smelling water mixed with oak bark or dung. This soaking tanned the skins and kept them from rotting. Later, when they were dry, they were dyed dark brown with the husks of walnuts.

What was this gift of the goats?

gathering walnut husks

It was leather, and it was ready.

The gold came from the rivers of Africa. It was carried on the backs of camels across the burning Sahara, north to Europe. There the soft metal was pounded flat and beaten under layers of strong paper until it was thinner than a blade of grass, more fragile than a butterfly's wing. This film of gold could now be stuck to paper or leather or turned into paint.

What had this gold,
shining like the sun,
become?

panning

for gold with a calabash

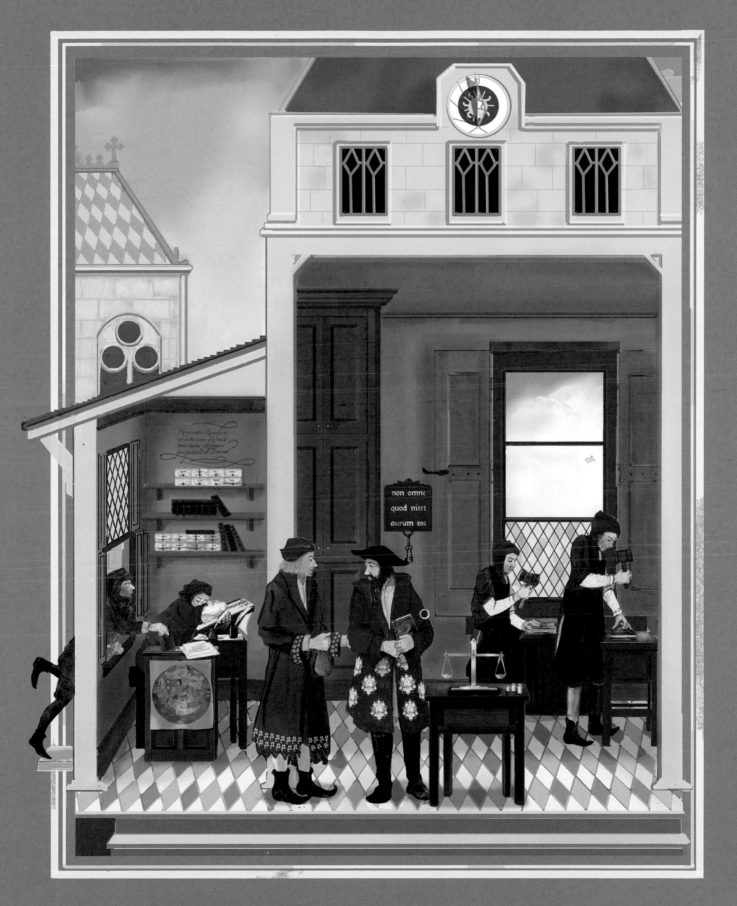

It had become gold leaf, and it was ready.

The seeds were gathered from the flax plant and crushed in a press. Out flowed a golden oil that was boiled until it was as thick as honey. Next pine tree pitch was burned under a bowl. The flames made a thick, black smoke that coated the inside of the bowl with soot. The soot was scraped off, mixed with the oil, and ground on a stone until soot and oil were smoother than butter, darker than night.

What was this sticky stuff that blackened everything it touched?

the flax plant

It was ink, and it was ready.

This is
the mold to make the letter Z.

The lead came from old pipes, the tin from old dented cups. The metals were melted with antimony powder until they shimmered like silver. The hot liquid was poured by the spoonful into a tiny mold. In a flash the liquid hardened. When the mould was opened, out fell a tiny piece of metal unlike anything anyone had seen before. On one end was a useless tail. It was snapped off. On the other a raised letter that faced backward. If the letter was an A, it was put in the A box. If a Z, it went with the Zs.

What were these letters shining like money?

They were printing types, and they were ready.

The oak came from a great tree that fell in a winter storm. The tree was hewn into logs and sawn into planks and hauled to the carpenter for measuring and cutting. The wood was planed and chiseled and hammered and carved and then assembled into a wooden machine with a wooden screw. The screw was smeared with grease and the wood was polished until it shone.

What was this machine as strong as a giant?

It was the printing press,
and it was ready.

A man from the Good Mountain in the city of Mainz made the ink and the type he would need. He designed the press and bought reams of paper. This man from the Good Mountain spent his nights thinking. He spent his days doing.

Who was this man?

He was Johannes Gutenberg,
"John from the Good Mountain," and he was ready.

He set the lead type into words,
then sentences, then whole pages.
He put the heavy metal pages
into the press.
He wiped his brow.

a page of set type—each letter faces backward

He opened the package of paper and dampened the sheets. Slowly the sheets softened as they swelled with water. He waited. He spread the ink out and, with two leather balls on handles, he daubed the ink onto the raised letters of the type. He took a deep breath.

type inked

He put a sheet of damp paper into the press and slid paper and type under the giant screw. He pulled the handle. The screw turned and pressed the paper onto the raised letters of the type. In a flash the paper was glistening with words. He looked at his work and smiled.

When printed, the type reads the right way.

The color red is made from the root of the madder plant.

The color blue is made from the lapis lazuli stone.

With his work finished, the Man from the Good Mountain took what he had printed to a little shop where an artist drew designs of flowers and birds and giant capital letters on some of the sheets. Another man painted in the designs with expensive colored powders he had mixed with oil and the sap of cherry trees. Then, carefully and patiently, a third man illuminated the designs with gold leaf, rubbing and polishing the metal until it glowed.

Yellow is made from the stamens of the saffron flower

In another room a man carefully folded the sheets and sewed them together. The sewn side was called the spine, which was made strong with glue. Next the sheets were trimmed, bound with paste, and sewn into two boards covered with leather. The work was now finished. The Man from the Good Mountain held what he had made in his hands.

What mysterious thing came from Mainz
that was made of rags and bones,
soot and seeds, covered in leather
and decorated with gold?
What did lead and tin, strong oak
and a mountain make?

A printed book,
not all that different from
the one you are holding,
and it would
change the world
forever.

Epilogue

Gutenberg changed the way books were made in Europe. Before him books were copied by hand. What Gutenberg did was invent a way to make copies with lightning speed. He found a way to cast letters in metal and print these letters on paper with a press. These ideas were revolutionary, and Gutenberg has been called the most influential man in the last one thousand years.

Gutenberg's books were works of beauty. The letters were crisp and clear. The ink was jet black, and even today it glistens like new. No one knows how he was able to do such beautiful work.

One of the books Gutenberg printed was the Bible. He made about 180 copies. Some he printed on paper and some on calfskin called vellum. About 47 copies have survived, but of these only 21 are complete. You can see a sample of his work in this book, on the page about bookbinding.

We don't know much about Gutenberg. He was born Johannes Gensfleisch in Mainz, probably around 1400.

When he was a young man, he added the name of his family home to his name: Gutenberg.

In those early years, he may have worked with precious metals like gold and silver.

He lived for a while in Strasbourg, France, where he invented things. We don't really know what these inventions were; perhaps they

No one knows how original Gutenberg's ideas were. Some of his ideas may have come from people working in the Netherlands and in other parts of Europe. But one thing is certain: after the 1450s, when Gutenberg made the first printed book, printed books were everywhere as people set up printing presses all over Europe.

From 1450 to 1500 printing was in its infancy. The books printed then have a special name to show how new they were: incunabula (in-kyoo-NA-byoo-la), which means "cloth in which you wrap a newborn baby."

For the next 500 years, the way books were made remained largely unchanged. There were certainly improvements. In the 1800s giant steam presses and mechanical typesetters were invented, and in the early 1900s electric-powered presses did much of the work. All the while, inventors were busy creating entirely new and faster ways to print words on paper so that books became cheaper and cheaper to make. By the 1980s

had something to do with printing. He may have printed religious souvenirs for pilgrims.

By 1448, he was back in Mainz, where he went into business with a man named Johann Fust. For a few years they worked together using Gutenberg's secret inventions to print books, perhaps in the Gutenberg family house. These books were the first to be printed in Europe using lead type.

Gutenberg may have remained single all his life, having neither wife nor children. He lived more than

Gutenberg home, no longer standing

sixty years and died in the winter of 1468. His grave disappeared long ago.

No one knows what he looked like. I chose to make him clean-shaven like most businessmen of the fifteenth century. I also gave him a head cloth or chaperon. This is not at all like the portraits you see of him showing a wise, strong man with a long, flowing beard. But then, these portraits were all painted in the sixteenth century, when beards were in style, long after Gutenberg had died.

computers began to take over much of the work. Yet even with all these changes, the pages were still printed with ink on paper and bound into books.

Not so today, for we are living in exciting times. The book as we know it is changing just as it did after 1450, when hand-copied books gave way to printed ones. Now printed books are giving way to e-books, and some say computers may one day make books made of ink and paper a thing of the past. Will all of tomorrow's books be made of silicon and light and be connected by the Internet to the world, or will they be something we can't even imagine today? So different will books be that fifty years from now, someone reading this book may wonder how it was made: how it used ground-up trees for paper, soy beans for ink, a plastic film to protect the cover, and a computer to set the type and print the pages. But that is another story: perhaps one you will write.

If you would like to know more, search these keywords on the Internet:

Gutenberg Museum Mainz, Laurens Janszoon Coster, Bi Sheng or Pi Sheng, the Gutenberg Project. Learn more about Gutenberg from the museum built in his honor. Some sites and many books you will come across may carry incorrect information because, over the centuries, people have made up all kinds of things about his life that cannot be proved. Learn about other inventors like Coster and Bi Sheng. Finally investigate a project that uses Gutenberg's name and makes books available on the Internet.

Widener Library, Beinecke Rare Book and Manuscript Library, Morgan Library and Museum, Library of Congress, New York Public Library, Scheide Library, Lilly Library, Huntington Library, Harry Ransom Humanities Research Center. These are all libraries and museums in the United States where you can see a complete or nearly complete copy of the Gutenberg Bible.

paper making, paper sizing, paper pulp, paper fibers, waterleaf paper. You will find how paper pulp is made. You will read about waterleaf and the role of sizing.

tannin, tanning leather, bookbinding. These words will lead you to information about the structure of a book and about a chemical in oak bark that prevents animal skins from rotting in the process of making leather.

gold leaf, manuscript, illumination, gold beaters, book of hours, saffron, madder, lapis lazuli, kermes, scriptorium, scribe. These words will take you to sites that tell why gold is so special and so valuable. You will also learn how and why people decorated their books with so much care and expense and how paint was made.

movable type, type metal, hand type casting, typography, type design, hand type setting, justification, leading, Otto Mergenthaler, kerning, typeface, type foundry, type font, anatomy/parts of foundry type, type case, California job case, history of printing, common press. Gutenberg put other metals into his type, not just lead. Learn about molds and matrices and what exacting work it is to design and make type. Discover the names of all the parts of a piece of foundry type. Find out how to hand set type and learn about mechanical typesetting. Learn about the hand press and see how it evolved into the massive machines used today. Also find out about printers today who still use the old methods of letterpress printing.

history of ink making, lampblack, copper oxide, flaxseed oil or linseed oil, nut oil, calcination. Gutenberg's inks were unique. Most ink makers used carbon gathered from soot, but Gutenberg may have added another kind of black powder, perhaps copper oxide. Some also say that Gutenberg may have used walnut oil instead of linseed oil. Read also how both oil and soot were purified to make the best ink.